The Lightness of Being Grounded

Ama

SYNERGY
PUBLISHING GROUP

BELMONT, NORTH CAROLINA

The Lightness of Being Grounded
Ama

Copyright ©2024 Ama. All rights reserved. No portion of this book may be reproduced in any form without permission from the author, except as permitted by U.S. copyright law. Contact the author at aproprose.press@gmail.com for permission requests.

Published by Synergy Publishing Group, Belmont, NC
Cover art by Kimberly Hanson
Formatting by Melisa Graham

Softcover ISBN 978-1-960892-30-0
E-book ISBN 978-1-960892-31-7

This book is dedicated to the me of December '22 who filmed a video of myself crying while bowing, with my hands wide open, asking for the way out.

Contents

Preface 1
Assignment 3
Love Is Lightning 7
Grounded in Desire 9
He Only Wants My Sunshine 11
FIRE 13
The Beach Part 1 17
Grounded 21
Heron 23
The Hotel: Grounding with Lies 25
Audre Lorde Question 27
The Beach Part 2 29
On Control 31
The Exit Door 35
On Brightness 37
The No-Contact Desert 39
Roots Survive 41
The Beach Part 3 45
A Little Bit on Dad and the sky 49
Grounding as Punishment 53

The Beach Part 4	55
Partnering	61
Vertical Freedom	65
Knots	67
On Lightness	69
My Fighter	71
Grounded in My Own Secret Language	73
The Beach Part 5	75
Love Poem To Me by Me	77
Family Judicial Court	81
Succulents	87
On Grace	89
Caught	91
The Beach Part 6	95
True Love	97
TRY	101
The Beach Part 7	103
The Lightness of Being Grounded	105
Epilogue	107
About the Author	109

Preface

Dear Reader,

In this book, I rip back the black sheets I used to cover my windows while my marriage fell apart in my wide open hands. I show you the inside of my home where it happened, and that home is simply my body. I uncover the hiding places where I'd kept the soft parts of myself, and I bring them back to the light.

This book is a mosaic of my experience persevering in a broken marriage, and then realizing the perseverance itself was the root of the pain. In the pages that follow, I fight with what it means to break a commitment, and then I finally break free. I hop on the bus, Gus.

In this book I explore what it means to re-center once you're uprooted. I discover that the way to break free from anything is, in fact, to ground down. I discover that pain, when honored, can turn into power. The earth is holding us close even when we don't realize it, and we are grounded even when we are free-falling.

Assignment

I have a friend who is a rolfer. Rolfing is a deep massage technique. My friend told me that sometimes, when she works on certain areas for her clients, they sob uncontrollably. She has come to expect this. As she massages their scapulas, wet tears materialize all over the massage table. She places both hands over the bone and holds herself still, while they cry and cry. They usually aren't able to explain where the sobbing is from, why the tears are flowing. Maybe it is because the sadness isn't tied to an event, not exactly. Instead, it is tied to a muscle or a nerve that they've wrapped up in an energy that they couldn't let go of from some other time ago. And now, with her massage, the emotion is finally being worked free.

I have another friend who is a masseuse. Part of her training was to go to the mall and watch how people walk when they are just existing in the world. Her teacher would tell her that by watching someone's gait, you can gain all the information you need about what's too tight, what's too loose, what will be in pain someday soon, or already is. Just by watching people, you can tell where they are holding their tension.

And still, I have another friend who went to DJ school with the goal of shaking people free. We befriended each other as dancers. We both learned how people hold themselves back from free movement because they think it's safer to be stuck. They think that you fall less when you hold back. They think that you're protecting yourself from injury if you remain tight. But the truth is, you create more injury by trying to protect yourself. Maybe you don't fall as much, but when you do, it's worse because of the tension you're holding. Now, as a DJ, she tries to bring people on a journey where they can let go of a little more of their holding, so they hurt less when they fall.

How resistant people can be to movement. How resistant we can be to shaking ourselves free, to dance. We hold ourselves tightly. We won't let others touch us. We won't even let ourselves touch us.

When you ask someone to dance, you see their limits. A veil is either lifted, or pulled quickly closed. The very best way to release a holding is movement, but you have to be *ready* to release it. Sometimes we pull the veil over our eyes so we can hold on a little longer. Some things we don't want to let go of. Ever.

What am I holding and why?
I am holding my children because they won't walk into daycare on their own.
I am holding my coffee cup long after the coffee is cold because
I am holding onto the hope that it's still hot.
I am holding my history because it justifies my behavior.

I am holding my breath.

I am holding my anger because I need it to fuel my resolve to move me forward.
I am holding myself close.
Holding my stomach in.
Holding my tears back.
Cradling my fears like they're fragile things I must not break.

What would happen if I opened my hands? What would happen if I shook it all up and out? Would I cry like the people on the rolfing table? And what would happen next?

It is terrifying to think of being empty. But if I were empty, I would have so much more capacity to feel full.

Love Is Lightning

The very first time I was swept up in love was on the floor of my closet in my childhood bedroom with a sweaty house phone pressed to my ear. The voice on the other end said something, and my entire body came alive with electricity. I could feel love spread like fire from my ear to my brain and then slide into my nervous system where it picked up speed and rushed through to my fingers and toes. I felt earth's gravity pulling me down and sticking me firmly to the floor, so drunk on the moment. So suddenly open.

The boy was a genius. At least I thought so. He was a D student because he wouldn't do his homework, but that was just rebellion, I thought. He'd sit in front of an assignment and refuse it. From where I sat on the complete opposite side of the English classroom, I saw his long straight blond hair, his absolutely ridiculous thick-rimmed glasses, his braces, and his defiance and was incredibly frustrated, which meant I thought about him more than any other boy. After class, he would slip me pages of poems. I would read them at night and think I'd been let in on a secret. This was the reason he was failing English—because he was "just too brilliant" for it.

The relationship was short-lived, as most young loves are. It was a flare in the middle of my adolescence that cemented the idea of love being lightning, and thunder being how it feels as that love finds its home inside my body.

I've moved through life looking for the hottest charge.

Grounded in Desire

I always call him when I feel hope. I don't know where the hope comes from exactly. It's me cooking dinner and suddenly thinking, *Maybe my husband has come back to himself today.*

I dial the phone with the hope that when we speak, it will be a little bit sweet and a little bit kind, with a little bit more understanding for each other. Maybe we will agree on something for once. Maybe he will be quick to offer a hand or some help with the kids. It's usually with a pure heart that I call him.

The thing about hope is it lives in the same place in my body as anxiety. They occupy the same nerve lines. They both look **forward** with their energy. Neither of them live in the moment.

I can say that I like the feeling of hope more than I like the feeling of anxiety, but both of them lead to the same place—the present. And sometimes the present that comes from hopefulness is a let down, and sometimes the present that comes from anxiety is a relief. But neither hope nor anxiety are grounded in the now. Instead, they are grounded in a desire.

This is something I do. I ground myself in my desires.
I am what I desperately want.

I am the me of the future who I can see so clearly and who I already love fiercely and who I can only dream of becoming. I am the me of an hour from now when my child wakes up and I vow to look at her, really look at her, and engage. I am the cup of coffee I'm about to get up and make, the little piece of sweet chocolate I will savor with it. I am the novelist I am working to become. I am sometimes, maybe most of the time, my hopes and my anxieties, and the nerves that carry both, grounded in a suspended state between the two.

What I desire is not always what I will get. He picks up the phone, and there is no love. My hopes dashed, my anxieties realized. I am momentarily weightless as I search for ground. In that suspended state is freedom—what do I want to happen next? What do I desire?

He Only Wants My Sunshine

He only wants my sunshine.
He wants me to tell him beautiful things.
He reaches out when it's too dark, but never at night. He reaches out when he's searching for sun,
his fingers walking the basement wall.

He wants me to talk like a poet about the rain so that he can bear the rain—
to tell him how I dipped my toes into the sporadic rain,
just the toes,
and how the cool put me
right to sleep.

He only wants my sunshine
because my darkness can match his darkness and together we would take the bullet.
He doesn't even want to know that I have it in me
to take a bullet.

I am really
more shadow than sunshine,
and more black blood than shadow.
But he only wants my sunshine.
I can't take anyone where they don't want to go.
That dark room is my own.

FIRE

The lights flicker just slightly. Something is disturbing the air. I can't really see it, but I can feel it if I close my eyes and think hard about my body. Maybe I can see it too, if I squint my eyes and look at the flickering light. It looks like turbulence, like waves. It could be as simple as the air conditioning cutting on, and the air moves, and the electricity responds, just so subtly.

I've always been aware of these little things. As a child, I went through periods of high anxiety. My first therapist told me it's because I could feel sensations in my body with more strength than others. If I was hungry, it would be amplified. If I was hot, it would become huge. When there's an open-ended question—*What is wrong with me?*—everything can make you anxious, but when you know that it's just messages from your own insides, you are able to get curious.

What is my body telling me right now that my mind cannot see? The lights flicker again.

An hour later, he is removing his things from the garage in grunts and slams. The wave was a foreshock, because now it's all here, and the lights everywhere are flickering.

You're told that if you get caught in a rip current, swim with it and out to sea until it "lets you go." If you fight your way toward shore, you will exhaust yourself and drown, so you have to trust that if you let yourself be taken and go with the flow, you will be released from the current and can swim back home. You're told this so that you know it.

But I know first hand that in moments of adrenaline and fear, the body takes over, and what you know doesn't mean anything. I have been ten feet high in aerial silks when my foot wrap went wrong, and suddenly I was knotted and couldn't get out, hanging high above a crowd. I knew how to untie the knot, but when the adrenaline is released into your bloodstream, knowing means nothing. You have to have muscle memory to untie yourself, to trust the current. You have to have practice.

I hear him screaming and slamming around. I cannot control this wave's turbulence. I'm told that even though I can't control the turbulence, I can control my own reactions. But knowing means nothing unless I've practiced.

The mastery of oneself—it can feel so impossible. To do nothing when everything inside of me wants to scream. I've described my emotions as heat that is right on the verge of burning me completely if I don't act, so I always act.

FIRE.

I am a fire sign—Leo. I am a fire dosha—pitta. I was born in a Chinese zodiac fire year.

I am built to burn.

If I could just sit still and not be afraid of the heat. I repeat,

Agni meele purohitam.
I surrender to the fire of transformation.

The lights flicker again.
Sit still, sit still, sit still.

Instead, I act.

And in the acting, I'm just fighting the current. I'm exhausting myself and drowning. I am already under water. I've already lost.

Agni meele purohitam.
I need to practice sitting still, so that next time, I think, NEXT TIME, I'll just let the fire burn until I'm all ash and smoke on the inside.
Smoldering and then nothing.
Next time.

The Beach Part 1

It's 9 a.m. on a Saturday when I wake up to tiny voices in the living room. The dog groans as I roll out of bed and climb over partially unpacked moving boxes that are blocking the door. Through the hall, I navigate a maze of more boxes and make it to the living room that's cluttered with piles of things. Books here, silverware there, a miscellaneous pile of toys and treasures.

The day before, it stormed for the entire five hour drive to our new home, and the rain seeped into the moving truck and soaked half of our boxes. The movers struggled to get them off the truck as the bottoms fell out and left a trail of wet cardboard and belongings throughout our house. That night, in the quiet of a new start, I piled everything in the living room to deal with later. Later is now.

I find the source of the voices. The two of them are huddled together on the couch around my son's tablet, watching science videos on YouTube. They are all skinny limbs and wild bedhead hair smooshed together to make one giggling organism.

"Morning," I say, as my daughter, just three and a half, jumps off the couch and dodges a pile of clothes to grab me around the waist.

"Hungryyyyy," she whines. I brush my hands over her hair and free myself from her grasp to search for breakfast.

We have leftover pizza, and that's all. I plug in the microwave, which is thankfully already on the kitchen counter, and toss some slices on paper towels. Back in the bedroom, I find the coffee machine and the beans packed away in boxes and get everything set up and brewing. The kids are giggling at something as I pass. It's good to hear them giggling. It's been a few months since they've sat together like this, relaxed and light.

Soon I join them, and then we're *all* relaxed and light, covered in pizza crumbs and little coffee spills, surrounded by our piles of stuff that made it here with us through all that rain.

By 11 we're restless. I've unpacked what I can, and the kids have explored the backyard, built a lego set, and run circles around my legs.

"We're going to the beach," I decide.

There's a flurry of excitement. Everyone's hands are in boxes pulling out clothes to find their warmest. It's January after all, and we're bundling up just so we can take off our shoes and feel the sand.

The drive out to the ocean is shorter than any of us expect, fifteen minutes total. It's scenic too, taking us over marshland with grass that's so bright green it pops against the blue sky. *I did it,* I think. *I have moved directly into the beauty, and I get to touch it every day.*

"I see the ocean!" my son yells as the clear blue water appears right in front of us in the cracks between two buildings. I don't know anything about this beach yet, so I drive along the stretch parallel to the shoreline until I find the first public parking sign I can. I pay the two dollars, and we're out in it. This is the fastest we've ever made it from decision to beach. Under thirty minutes to see the ocean.

The wind is ferocious. We aren't prepared, and our ears burn with the cold air whipping past. The sand is kicked up in swirls around our ankles, gathering in tiny piles in the crevices of my rolled up pants. Sandy, windy, cold.

We do not care.

My children run straight for the water, throwing their arms out wide and becoming as big as the shoreline. I kick off my shoes and dig my toes into the cold sand.

We are the only ones on the beach, bundled up in thick down coats, but after my son and daughter have run in a million tiny circles, they throw off their coats and let the wind a little closer in. I've always hated the cold, but I do not hate it here. The pelicans fly in lines above our heads. I am breathing so easily.

Finally.

Grounded

My body is a dancer.

It has been dancing long before I danced it. As a tiny, six-year-old actress reciting words on a stage, my body would sway to the lyrical sound of the lines. It would push its chest forward to seem bigger than it was when the character required confidence. It would make itself incredibly small and hide in a corner when it needed to be inconspicuous. As I grew, my friends would dare me to squeeze into tiny spaces just to watch my body dance itself small. They would dare me to be silly in front of strangers just to watch my body dance itself loud.

My body is petite—at full height, it is only five-foot-two, but it has been dancing its way to eye level with every other body it encounters. I have never felt short inside this body. I have always managed to match what other people give, because my body is a dancer. It can even grow outside of itself. From somewhere on the inside, it can project itself outside itself and dance with the air current, or the feeling current, or the mood. In this way, my body can be light. It can float. Just like a traditional dancer that can seemingly levitate, my body can dance this way too.

My body dances down. It has done this from birth because gravity makes all of our bodies do this. But beyond that "down," childhood-me ran around in bare feet—I called them better feet—so my body could dance its roots into the earth with each step.

My feet, I have been told, are what everyone watches when I dance my own body. My feet, I have been told, look like they are kissing the floor, and everything that happens with the rest of my body above looks like the energy released from the kiss.

Dance, as an art form, came to me because my body was already doing it. Every day when it walked through the halls of my middle school and demanded or rejected attention, I was dancing.

One of the first things they teach you in modern dance is how to release into the floor. Much time is spent lying on the floor and intentionally letting your weight fall down as completely as you can while your teacher says, "Feel the floor supporting your weight." What they're doing is grounding you. They are not just grounding your body; they are preparing you to trust that you are grounded. That's because the next step is learning how to fall.

Dancing IS falling. You fall into momentum. You fall through the space. You fall down to the floor. You fall into your partner.

The falling comes from the trust built from the grounding. A teacher once told me, "You can only go as far as the floor."

Heron

Last night, I dreamt he had a shotgun with birdshot. He shot it high into the air. Then a flock of blue heron flew up from the brush, low and powerful.

I screamed, "Do not shoot those birds!"

He hesitated, then turned back and started taking them down.

Their beautiful blue bodies fell like soft paper from the sky.

The Hotel: Grounding with Lies

The lawyer told me to go back and find all the evidence. So I started to go back ....

I am looking for all of the evidence in a sea of endless evidence, scrolling to find the worst thing. This is the worst one. This. This one. But this one is worse. Videos and voice memos and a novel of texts. All these words that hurt me so deeply, that put me in such a state of sorrow and put me on my knees at Christmas, crying into the pile of presents I'd meticulously wrapped ....

My lawyer told me that I need to present an even account. A fair account. So I look for my flaws in it. Sometimes I lost my patience and yelled for him to leave. Sometimes I yelled with a child in my arms. Sometimes I picked up every child I could carry and left the house. My children got very quick at packing bags. We only used them once.

That one time when we went to a hotel right before bedtime. There were just two of them then, and I was pregnant. The hotel was three miles away from my house, and I spent a fortune to spend a single night there. I told them we were having an adventure, and I tried to make it seem so fun, but when we got there, the room was small and dark and lonely with two tiny beds and a window that looked out over the parking lot. "Check out that view!" I laughed, but I don't think they thought it was funny.

I put on a Disney movie, and we all fell asleep in one bed. My phone vibrated all night with him trying to reach me, but I had given us a night away from the screaming, and I honored that for them. I wrapped my arms around my two blondies who'd gotten so tall since the last time I wrapped them up this way, and I let our heartbeats synchronize. Three children stabilized by their one resilient mother.

In the morning, we had continental breakfast, and I searched through our suitcases for toiletries, which all of us had forgotten. I thought about going to Target, but I didn't think I could convince them that any other part of this fleeing was "such a fun adventure." I wanted a shower, and they wanted their electronics and their toys, and they didn't want to run around a tiny, depressing room I'd promised would be "fun" for another second.

So we went home, back into the screaming. Back into the vibration and the buzzing and the tension. One night in a hotel, reminding us that we were the unit.

That I was the beacon.

It would be another two years before I would light the way out.

Audre Lorde Question

What are the words you do not yet have?

I do not yet have words for how it feels to be inside a body when it is being attacked. I don't have words yet for the way my chest sinks and how it pulls everything around it like a black hole.

I don't know how to tell you what it means to be willing to take a bullet versus being shot. One is a sacrifice; the other is an assault.

I don't yet have words to explain how, over time, my face lost its shine, my eyes became dark from crying, and how that looks in the mirror. Sorrow and age both appearing at once.

I don't yet have words for why I stayed or for what it takes to break away because I haven't done it yet—not completely. I cannot seem to drag myself back far enough from the invisible bind to snap the tie and take myself home.

I don't yet have words for the loneliness I can feel on the other side of this, how I can reach my hand across the barrier and touch it and how consuming it feels, and terrifying, and I know it's coming.

I don't yet have words for how home would feel now, or even where it lives.

The Beach Part 2

We learn that a winter beach walk must always include a hat that covers your ears. We learn that, at high tide, the left side of the beach is completely devoid of walkable sand. We learn how to park in the free spaces in residential areas with all four tires off the road. We learn to take the backroads, to cut out the beach traffic, to watch the pedestrian crossing at every block. We learn that if you go to the right and drive as far as you can, then walk another thirty minutes you'll be at the tip of the peninsula where the marsh and the ocean merge in a crash of water, all disagreeing on which way to flow. This place looks like a mohawk of waves for as far as you can see, like a dragon's tail. We learn to keep a jug of water in the back of the car to wash our feet of sand. I refill the jug the moment I get home, so it's always there whenever we decide on a forty-five minute beach trip. We learn that forty-five minutes can be enough to lighten our hearts.

One day, close to the dragon's tail, we find a little tide pool. My son leans down and picks up the tiniest hermit crab I've ever seen. How did he even see it? When we look closer, we see hundreds of them, all clicking their antennas, climbing on top of each other. They are in shells that are smaller than my fingernails, and the kids hold them in their open palms and watch them crawl around.

A few years prior, on a family beach trip, I bought a hermit crab from one of those boxy surf shops. I brought it home in a plastic container with a pink lid. The shop gave me a sponge and a water dish and sent me on my way. *Here's a live creature for you to figure out. Water it. Good luck.*

In the days that followed I researched everything there is to know about caring for hermit crabs. I learned they are very social and will usually die in isolation if they don't have friends. In the wild, they live in large communities, and switch shells as a group, lining up from largest to smallest and trading down the line. They chirp and click at each other to communicate. They breathe water from the air through gills, so must live in very humid environments, and they bury themselves in substrate to molt—often being mistaken by their owners as dead and thrown out at their most vulnerable. This quick buy for $3.00 at the surf shop was actually an incredibly complex creature with incredibly complex needs.

I got my hermit crab a few friends, *as many as can be kept in the tank* per the articles I'd read, and when they disappeared under the sand, I left them for months. Unfortunately my little pets didn't survive more than a year. I did my very best for them, but certain complex things cannot be kept well.

At the beach, we spend hours with our feet in the tide pool, holding the wild hermit crabs. They move their antennae at us. Their shells are perfect spirals. We gently place them back in the water, making sure none have climbed on our toes before moving on.

On Control

When you're taught about the body, you learn that one knot of tension in the shoulder can jut the opposite hip out of alignment, can send the spine in a swirl, can make it impossible to lift the leg. You learn that one outstretched toe can pull every bone, from tip to top, into a straight line. You start to see the connections, all the sinew, all the nerves, spread across space like a map. When you get good at seeing the connections, you get good at control.

Getting good at control can sometimes look like making a clean seam in a folded towel, but it can also look like effortlessness as you learn to mask the control. When you've mastered control, it looks like ease.

That is how I tricked him, he said. I made it look so easy, so effortless, so light. That's what they've all said.

Except when you peel back the layers, you see that the weightlessness is a trick.

Beauty in the natural world is random. Accidental, even. It's a sudden moment of sunset that you don't expect, a silence that comes across a marsh and you just happen to catch it. Beauty is my brother with a pencil in his hand, his bunched up forehead as he's focusing on his drawing. It is random.

If you want to capture and showcase that beauty, you have to use your hands to collect it in a box, and then let it shine out just a little at a time. You have to use control.

"You're so controlling." "You did it to be in control." "You lie so you can keep your control." "You have to stay in control." "You'll get everything just how you want it."

I've heard it said that time is a spiral. It's not a line, and it's not a looping circle, but it spirals back on itself, confronting you again and again with the same lessons to see how far you've grown.

I say this to myself now, while I'm squeezing in a shower after making four different breakfasts for four different children, with a twenty-minute window to get them to the bus. "Time is not linear. It's a spiral," I say as I half-ass wash my hair, rush a quick body wash, and then stand still under the hot water wishing I could just stay there in the heat and warmth and wet. "Time is not linear. It's a construct," I say as I try to space out the seconds before I have to face the cold and face the kids.

I've been trying to wake up and present myself. I've been trying on a skin care routine, trying on getting dressed, trying on makeup. Today, I tried to put on bright purple lipstick, and my two older kids smiled and told me I looked like a flower.

These things we do for ourselves, small treats of love we give to our bodies, are not easy to do in the middle of a separation. Who chooses this? Who chooses a separation?

Someone who has come up against how little control she actually has.

Beauty is random. It is an accident. You can control it in a box for a little while, shining only a little out at a time, but even if you don't catch it and contain it, it will show up all on it's own.

I loosen my grip.

I kiss my kids with my purple lipstick until we all look like flowers.

The Exit Door

The night he punched the television, the electricity sparked in a rainbow, and the whole room was so bright and colorful and brilliant before it went pitch black.

He slammed the bedroom door, and in the silence that was left, I saw that the door frame had splintered. When I knew he wasn't coming back, I snuck over and broke off a shard of wood. I kept it in my pocket, touching the rough edges when I needed a reminder that I could also be a sharp edge.

Then one day in February, I saw the exit door. It cracked open while he was out of town, and I pulled the splinter from my pocket and wedged it in before the door closed.

Every day he stayed away, I pried the door open just a little wider until I could get us all out.

And then *somehow*
through every single heartbreaking moment
and every single chord that fought not to be cut
and every single hope that did not want to die
I stayed out.

I don't even know how I'm still out.

Walking through the door felt like breaking something sacred.
But it wasn't sacred.

The rainbow arc of the television was momentarily beautiful before it settled in the deep darkness, but it originated from violence, and it ended in emptiness.

A single moment of beauty isn't enough to call something sacred.
Just because something is fleeting doesn't make it precious.

The truth is, he **HATED** me.
I've never known someone to hate me so thoroughly.
So **SHARPLY**.
I didn't think hate like that could even **COME** from love.
I always thought love would buffer it somehow.
Make it softer.
Make it more like hurting
and less like rage.

On Brightness

When you become light, you create shadows.
When you are at your brightest, it *hurts*.

You and everyone.
They can't even look at you.
They cannot take the way they look in the fullness of you,
and your skin is on fire, and it hurts.

Pain and pleasure feel the same.
Brightest light and darkest shadow feel the same.
Love and Hate feel the same.
Everything in the extreme is just
Extreme.

I have come from the dark shadow and now I stand in my bright light
and I shine and shine
and wait for it to feel different—like happiness. Like joy.
Like breathing.
But it doesn't.
I have picked myself up from the ground and I stand on the tallest
pedestal and I wait for the pleasure,
but it's pain.

He has cried into the phone, and I want to embrace him.
And I wonder what it is in me that honors other people's pain above
my own?

The No-Contact Desert

There is a desert named No-Contact. I stand on one side and wonder how I'm ever going to cross. At the edge of the desert, there is a breeze. There is a hint of calm. It betrays the stretch before it and how difficult it might be. I stand there with it all stretching out before me and clutch my phone in my hands and dial his number over and over again. Each number is a little drop of water, and I swallow it and dial it again and again.

Staring at the desert, the little drops of water are everything. The breeze and the water, why would I leave? I dial again, a drop. Again, a drop. I could live this way, hydrated and cool, staring down the desert and choosing not to step one single foot inside of it.

But each number is *just* a single drop. Each drop dissolves as quickly as it's in my mouth, and I am left needing another. There is nothing to truly quench my thirst. If I stay here, dialing, I will actually die thinking that I am keeping myself alive.
And if the number connects ...

All of the little drops of water come right back out. From my sweat or my heat or my eyes—and the tears fall to the ground.

The choice seems simple. I need to step into the desert
and go.

I don't want to do it. I want to stay with the tease of water and the tricky breeze that makes me feel almost alive.

I look around for anything at all,
anything
that can transform these little bits of water into rain.

If I scream loud enough or fight hard enough or am more creative or more resourceful or explain myself better or reframe it in my mind.

I am a powerhouse, and that means I can certainly trick myself
into anything
and reason anything
and tell the deepest lies that weave themselves into almost truths,
so close to truths,
if they just weren't lies they would be
True.

They are not true. The truth is, I am dying on the edge of a desert and calling it living.

The choice seems simple. I need to step into the desert
and go.

Roots Survive

A few weeks after he moved out, two men came to cut down a pine tree in the backyard. He'd scheduled it months prior and forgot to cancel, so one warm Tuesday, they were at my front door with their chainsaws and harnesses, asking for access to the back.

They spent an entire eight hours slicing up the twenty-foot tree. We watched with fascination from the living room window as one man climbed to the top as if he were simply walking up the tree. They cut the branches first. Looking up at the tree, the branches don't seem as big as they are, but once they're on the ground, you realize just how massive they are. The branches fell where they wanted and came down with a brushing sound, almost like wind. Soon, no one could step through the backyard without having to climb. I watched the one man who stood on the ground try to maneuver his body around branches. He found a small space just large enough for his body, and tried to stand his ground, as pine needles fell from the sky. The sound of the chainsaw continued.

Eventually, the men were on the trunk. The man at the top of the tree would lower himself just enough, and would cut a chunk of the tree at a time. The man on the ground used a pulley system they'd built to try and lower the trunk piece to the ground. The weight of each piece was at the mercy of gravity though, and his pulley did barely anything. Each chunk of the trunk would hit the ground with a resounding THUD. It rumbled inside our chests as we watched from the window.

Hours later, the tree was down, and my backyard was an obstacle course of thick trunk and long cumbersome branches. The men left the mess with me.

He'd moved out, and in his wake, he'd left a twenty-foot pine in pieces in the backyard.

The tree had been alive and healthy, and the cutting had been to create enough sunlight in the backyard to garden. The tree still seemed alive even though it was cut to pieces. Bugs crawled through the bark, and it oozed some kind of thick liquid sap; it still felt like it was bleeding. It felt this way for weeks on the ground of my backyard, and I would go out and sit with it.

Recently, I heard the description of a tree trunk being full of woody tissue. Tissue. As if wood can be delicate like tissue paper or fold the way human tissue folds. As if wood is not a solid thing, the way I consider it to be, but something full of fluid or full of movement or able to flow. Able to breathe.

It's been eight months since the tree was cut. The branches were pulled into a fire pit and burnt with the help of tons of gasoline (to burn up the moisture still within them). The pinecones were raked into a pile and thrown over the fence. The pieces of trunk were chainsawed down to manageable pieces and rolled out of the way. They still sit in the backyard, waiting for me to heft them some other place. The tree is still there as a trunk, as a root system, that is probably bigger than the branches were themselves.

I wonder sometimes, if we could pull the roots up, how much of the yard would come with them? You can cut down every visible piece of a tree, but what happens to the things you can't see? Do roots shrivel up and decompose all on their own? Or do they stay right where they are, suspended deep in the earth with all of the untapped potential that was cut off at the tip. Do they keep sending signals, as I know they did when the tree was alive? Do they keep shooting out electricity to warn every other tree? *I was a beautiful twenty-foot pine tree. They destroyed every part they could see. The only safe thing is what you can hide. Put your energy into your roots. It's the part that will survive.*

The Beach Part 3

A month later, it's 9 a.m. on a Monday when we learn the beaches have been closed. Covid restrictions had already closed down the restaurants and malls, but the beaches are shut down now too. *In an effort to protect our beach communities,* the order says.

My children and I walk in circles in the yard for a few days. We sunbathe in a tiny section of grass. We dance in bathing suits in the afternoon. But the novelty of being bored together wears off fast, and we start to snap at each other. I start a workout routine to burn off some of my energy. I try to organize their day with chores to give them some structure, yet there is only so much you can do when you can't leave the house—everyone reading this understands.

We are also the beach community, I think. *We are only fifteen minutes from the beach!*

"Shoes on!" I yell, and the kids don't even move from their positions on the couch. "Come on, let's go!"

"Where?" my son says, not even looking up from his tablet.

"We're going to the beach."

"Closed" my littlest says, still not moving.

"We're going anyway," I say. "Shoes on."

Through the local news outlets I know that if you don't live a certain radius from the beach and you're caught on it during lockdown, you get fined, but I'm willing to risk it. I moved here to see the ocean every day, and I'm going to. We stash our masks in our pockets and leave, the excitement of being rebelliously free during lockdown buzzing inside me.

The roads are practically empty. This doesn't seem too shocking to me since I'm still fairly new to the town, and it will still be another year before I see what beach traffic really looks like outside of a pandemic. I blast music, and the children dance in the backseat.

We come to the bridge just before the beach and see three people standing beside the road with cardboard signs. "Don't Come Here" one says in huge black sharpie letters. "The Beach Is Closed" is written on another. The people are masked and standing far away from each other, waving their signs around at our car. It feels dystopian, like something I've seen in a zombie movie. It's early yet in the pandemic, and I haven't gotten used to not seeing people's mouths, so I try to see their eyes as we pass. They look like they're shooting lasers at us.

"Mom?" my son says, nervous from the back seat.

"We are just normal people getting home from the grocery store," I say. "How do they know we don't live here?" I forge ahead with a singular focus: get my children away from our tiny backyard and into the fresh ocean air. We aren't a danger. We haven't even left our home in days. We just want to walk on the beach.

We get to the beach and park on a side street. "As if we're visiting family," I remind them, and I take a deep breath as I unlock the doors. We look both ways for signs of people before exiting the car, but the streets are empty. No one is driving or walking or sitting on their porch. Everything is silent, just like in a zombie movie. We walk tensely away from the car, abandoning it quickly, so no one can pinpoint where we came from, and don't relax until we have the beach in our sights. But the moment we see the ocean …

The beach is empty too. No one is there. If I lived on the shore, I don't know how I could resist this vast space. This breeze. This blue sky with v-lines of pelicans that soar overhead. I have never before been on a beach devoid of all people, but it is so calm. Both children run straight for the shore and get their feet wet. They dig their hands down into the sand and get covered from head to toe. I sit down and watch them. Free. In wide open air.

How does anyone own this? I think. *How does anyone own it enough to shut others out from it? And if someone does actually own it, how can it be me?*

After an hour, we gather ourselves up and start the walk back to the car, but the moment we see the road, we see a white pickup truck parked on it, waiting for us. I tell the kids to keep walking as if we're just going home, but the officer rolls down his window and motions for me to come over. He has a black mask on, so I pull mine out of my pocket and cover my face as I approach.

"The beach is closed," he says.

"We are just heading home," I say, not technically lying.

"Do you live here?"

"Just visiting," I say again, still not technically lying.

"If you don't live here, you can't come here right now. You'll get a ticket."

My initial thoughts are of frustration. How can someone kick me out of an open space? How can someone say I cannot touch the sand that is public sand, or look at the ocean that is wild enough that it cannot belong to any person? I want to tell this cop to fuck off. But I have enough sense to take a breath and grab my children's hands. I remember what a friend once told me about interactions with officers—ask them their name because it throws them off guard. They consider, just for a split second, who you are and who you know and if they're in the right to stop you after all.

"What's your name, officer?"

Just like my friend said, the cop hesitates. If I wasn't watching, I would have missed it. My children huddle behind me, trusting me here because there's nothing else to do.

"Officer Patton," he says.

"Well Officer Patton. Thank you for reminding us of the policy. Have a good day," I say, and I march my children away from the pick up. Officer Patton lets us go. He doesn't demand I come back, and he doesn't follow us to see where we're going. He stays parked in his truck, watching us walk away. We get a block over and see our car and break into a run, flinging open the doors and buckling into our seatbelts. Before long the signs are waving in the rearview mirror. "The Beach is Closed."

A Little Bit on Dad and the sky

This morning, I walked outside to heat up the car and saw the kids' bikes left out from the night before, wet. The night before, the forecast showed zero percent chance of rain. This morning, the bikes were soaked. I looked up at the sky as if to say, seriously? But I saw a cloud parting and the sun shining through, and this beautiful pink and orange color on its outline, and the first thought I had was of my father.

Fourteen years ago, at a ripe age of fifty-six, he passed away before the sun came up. That morning when I drove away from the hospital, I was driving into the sunrise. It was pink and orange everywhere, stretched out against this baby-blue fresh-morning color. Wisps of white clouds peppered the sky with texture. It was beautiful.

I think I was crying in my car; it's been so long. I think I was saying *Daddy* over and over again. I was thinking about his soul split into a thousand pieces and merged with all of the colors in that crisp sunrise sky.

My dad, when he was alive, was my heart. He was a flawed man, and we had a flawed relationship, made even more so in his death as I learned about who he was as a person, but none of his flaws mattered at all to me. Not a single one.

My father was only my heart, and the morning of his death my heart was split into a thousand pieces and merged with all the colors in that crisp sunrise sky.

In the afternoon after he passed, my brother showed me a piece of paper he'd torn from the EKG machine that had beeped incessantly beside us to show my father's gradual decline and eventual death. It was a print out of my dad's heartbeat.

We went straight to a tattoo shop and each got the jagged lines etched into our skin, mine on my arm and my brother's on his chest. My dad was my heart, and now I had his, forever on my sleeve.

Years later, a doctor at a bar saw my tattoo and told me that one of the atria was broken.

"See this small line next to that big one? That shows that the left chamber is failing. Did he die of heart failure?"

"No," I said. "Heartbreak."

My dad died of heartbreak, and now I have his flawed heart on my arm. But it is *his,* and therefore, the flaws don't mean anything. The *heart* part negates all the other parts. I have his heart.

This morning, the little patch of sky with its pink and orange took me right back to that morning, when my father was in the sky. Fourteen years ago bumped into now in a collision so powerful it made me, busy me, pause.

"Hi, Dad," I said, and I breathed in the oxygen that surrounds us, the fragility of our lives, the silliness of our stress and our sadness, the heaviness of our humanness and grief.

How lovely to be alive. How tragic. How lovely. How tragic. How lovely.

Grounding as Punishment

"He's grounded, right?"—my son's father via text.
"What does that even mean?" I reply.

Despite sitting here day after day and contemplating the concept of grounding, I still don't know what "grounded" means in the context of punishing others.

How do you ground a generation that doesn't really go anywhere? He's BEEN grounded. Grounded in the backyard where he spends most of his time creating imaginary worlds. Grounded in the house where he's working on a creative project on his computer or making a comic book.

What was the point of grounding? Stay in one place, child. Ground yourself in the rules of the family, the expectations from your parents.

Grounding as a consequence?

My generation has spent the majority of the last ten years shimmying out of the expectations of others. We've been cutting people out, walking away, focusing on finding a community that helps us reach the potential we, ourselves, want to achieve. Not what our parents wanted. Not the rules of our family. We've been freeing ourselves from anything preventing us from being ourselves.

Grounding can be used as punishment—maybe—but I only correlate the two when it is self-punishment: Grounding yourself in a lie. Grounding yourself in the false idea that someone else will save you from whatever pain you're in.

The Beach Part 4

For the rest of lockdown, I make it an adventure to sneak onto the beach. I take the kids to different beaches, park in different places, sneak on in different ways. I find a bike path that takes us through a private community and golf course. We park at an abandoned administrative building and unload the bikes to embark. The path winds through deep woods, by marshes and small lakes, past huge alligators that lounge in shallow water, but if we keep biking far enough, the path opens onto a residential road that runs parallel to the beach. This becomes a regular adventure. Park the car, bike for an hour, jump in the ocean, bike back. We see no one for weeks this way. The kids name the alligators by size and general location. My daughter masters riding a bike without training wheels. We have an unmonitored beach to ourselves.

We do not take it for granted. Every day we can, we are out on it, slamming our bodies with the waves. We let the beach tan our skin, the salt water mat our hair, the sand come home in the car.

A month later, at 9 a.m. on a Monday the governor lifts the restrictions, and the public is allowed back to the beach. I had already felt it coming with the growing road traffic as people went back to work and back to see friends. No one could stay safe and inside forever.

On this Monday though, the news comes that I have lost my secret beach trips. *At least the kids will feel more comfortable*, I think. My son could never quite get behind the breaking of the law, always a little anxious as we ran away from the car. He'd relax at the beach as we all did, but would always ask me, "Are we okay?" when we finally drove away from our secret parking spot.

We venture out as free agents to go to the beach close to home. On this day, we turn left instead of right, and we drive as far as we can to find something new. We'd become intimate with the right side of the peninsula, but what's hiding on the left?

We park the car and watch the people around us. They aren't going to the public beach access at the front of the parking lot, but are instead crossing a barrier and walking down a closed road that leads even farther left. We follow. The road, having not been driven on in however long, is smooth and flat without potholes or blemishes, but covered in graffiti. It stretches as far as we can see, and every inch of it is spray-painted. The people who walk in front of us are walking in silence, as if drawn left by some other force. They drag their feet a little as they keep pace. The scene looks like a cliché road to heaven, but with the dark undertones of spray-painted humanity along the path. "I'll show you a good time," one tag says, with a cell number underneath, or there's a picture of a girl hiking her skirt above the knee. There's other tags too, innocent graffiti names drawn quick and sharp. A sunshine with a smiling face. A moon and star.

The kids and I walk in silence because it seems like the thing everyone is doing as if this is a place to treat with reverence despite its crude or messy graffiti. But the truth is it's buggy. Gnats are eating our arms and legs. Black flies are taking bites. My daughter keeps jumping from side to side to avoid the mosquitos that are attacking her legs, while my son runs ahead to try and escape the swarms.

We bring bug spray when we go left, I take note.

The road opens up onto a small sand path, and the mosquitos intensify. We follow the line of people, slowed down by the change in sand and the sudden uphill climb. When I look up again, I see the beach opening up suddenly before us. It is not just a straight line of shore either. There's texture.

The remnants of an old building stand, half submerged in water and covered in graffiti. A group of teenagers sit on the walls with their feet dangling into the sea. Over to the left are old trees buried in sand, their bark smooth, leaning out toward the sea. We are standing on sand, but in front of us is a section of small rocky pebbles, and the waves roll over them making little clinking noises.

The stones remind me of the rocky beaches in Portugal. When I walked on the beach there, the bottoms of my feet were prodded and massaged by the smooth ocean rocks. When the salt water rolled over them, they were peach, red, seafoam green, luminous. I brought rocks back from that beach in my pocket and gifted them to my family that Christmas, but by the time we were back in the US, the colors were gone. I'd instructed the family to run the rocks under water or put them in their sinks as decorations, but I'm not sure they ever got back the shine they had on the beaches in Portugal.

Here, the rocks are not colorful, but they are texture nonetheless. This beach has a ton to see. The kids and I explore the old building, as the teenagers ignore us. We step over the rocks. We climb the trees. Beyond the trees I see more beach with marsh grass growing right out of the sand. I yell for the kids to follow and climb farther over more protruding trees. A puppy runs up and sniffs my arm and

I look for his owner. There's a group of twenty-somethings gathered a little ways off the beach, in the thick of the smooth bark trees.

"Sorry!" a guy with long hair says, and he runs to retrieve the puppy.

My daughter laughs as the puppy licks her face and jumps on her. They fall in a playful puddle on the sand. The guy finally pulls his puppy away and back to his group. Someone is playing a guitar, and a few people are dancing around. The puppy jumps up and down at the dancer's feet.

We move on until we are on a tiny strip of sand. On one side is the ocean, but on the other is the marsh. Both are closing in on the strip as if soon they will swallow the entire piece of land completely. I momentarily wonder if I'm going to strand us on a sandbar, but I see a few adventurous couples farther up the shore, where there is a little more peninsula, and we press on. To our right, an old lighthouse stands in what looks like the middle of the ocean, on just enough sand for its base.

We are almost at the end of the peninsula, and the couples in front of us have disappeared somewhere. I sit down in the sand to signal this is as far as we will go. The afternoon is dissolving into evening, and the sky is starting to shift toward sunset. My son comes to sit beside me, and my daughter dances in circles on the small strip of sand to our right. I notice the birds. Since moving here, I've noticed the birds with long white legs, the egrets and cranes, the seagulls of course, the grackles that sounds like robots when they sing, the cormorants that swim submerged in water with their necks above water in the shape of the lochness monster. These birds are different. They are tiny and white. They are birds that I would usually not pay attention to. Just a bird. But as my son and I sit there and my daughter dances beside us, I watch them flock out over the ocean and back to the shore. Back and forth they go, out and in, out and in. More birds come the longer we sit, until there's a crowd of them flying in spiraling circles.

"Mom, look," my son says, getting up and walking to a sign behind us. "It's a bird sanctuary."

Sure enough, we are sitting right in front of a cordoned off section of the peninsula, simple string and stakes keeping humans from trampling across what I now see are nests made directly in the sand from tiny piles of shells. *Plover*, the sign calls them. This is where they nest.

The little plovers continue their out and back flocking as the sun starts to set. We have been out here for over an hour watching them as the sky starts to color. A few at a time, they fly over our heads to their nests. With light fading fast, I start to walk the kids back along the shore. The tide has gone out and left us with a little more beach, but we are still making our way on barely any sand. We get to the smooth bark trees and climb over. The group of people with the puppy have lit a small bonfire, and there's singing. It's comforting to have these kinds of people around, who have nothing else to do but spend an entire afternoon and evening nestled in the beach trees with a guitar and a puppy.

Partnering

And what of the ungrounded? What of the floating? The flying? The high? What of the feeling of trusting that someone else will carry you across the finish line?

Once I went out in an ocean kayak with a friend. There was a spider in the boat, and I had a miniature freak-out and flipped the thing, way out past the wave break. I was unexpectedly unstable in a way I'd never been before. My toes reached down to find the ground to flip the kayak back, but there was no ground. At one point, I intentionally went under to see how far from the bottom I was, but it was farther than I was willing to go. What could I do out there in the ocean without any ground? Luckily my kayak partner had been here before, and he was able to flip us back over and pull me in. The spider was gone, and I felt a side dish of guilt along with my main course of humility.

In romance lately, I have intentionally tried to put my trust in others after being told that I have a hard time releasing control. I've considered this in each new relationship, and I've tried to release my grip and trust that someone else is there to catch what I drop, but I have misjudged what someone else can carry, and they have misjudged it too. I have been too heavy for the people I've asked to carry me, and I have ended up in the river searching for the sediment on the bottom with outstretched toes while the current carries me downstream.

In partner dancing, you learn to "hold your weight," which means activating your muscles in a way that makes you feel lighter to lift. I hated being lifted because even when I carried my weight, I was heavier than the rest. I was strong, dense, powerful, and difficult to lift. I always felt the effects of someone who was not ready for how heavy I was.

In partner dancing, you learn not to "dump down," which means not to relax your body. Don't give someone your full weight because they cannot lift you when you are dead weight. Don't succumb to gravity. Don't relax. Don't give in.

There is another kind of partner dancing—contact improvisation. This kind of dancing is about finding a contact point of shared weight. You start to learn contact improv by putting your hands together, or one person holding the other's arm, and you practice "giving all of your weight."

After learning how to hold your weight, it is a great unlearning to release everything you have into someone else. I have to close my eyes and think "down." When you give yourself this way, a balance point is created. The trick is that you are both giving completely. If one person is holding, it makes the transitions clunky, and the other person cannot find the leverage to lift and move and slide. You must both give, and you must both relax. This creates freedom.

So you can hold.
You can carry your weight.
You can keep it yourself.
You can even find freedom this way.

Or you can find the partner who can give their weight completely,
and you can challenge yourself to do the same,
knowing that the only way this results in freedom is if there's
equal effort.

Vertical Freedom

I am watching the expansive sky. So blue. Really it's clear. Really it's air. Really it's no color. Really it's every color split up and spread out all at once. Boundless and open and full and empty.

Who we are is just like this. We are a scattering of all we've been taught and all we believe to be true and the few experiences that have hooked themselves into our fleshy bodies and won't shake free. Some things dissipate faster than others, and the things left behind are "me."

We look up and say "how blue." We look inside and say "I."

Maybe one day humans will understand that we are the same thing as the sky and we can, at any time, close our eyes and become it.

The first time I flew in a small plane, my uncle's little red puddle jumper, the concept of vertical freedom took hold. When driving, you know that you are moving across the ground, which is a flat surface. But in a plane, there are no boundaries and no concept of flat. Two things could fly in the same place in a different vertical plane—and you may be saying "of course," but feeling it is different than knowing it. And knowing it is different, still, than a large passenger plane that tracks its vertical incline and flattens out along an invisible road to keep you comfortable and in-line with your expectations of traveling. In a little plane like my uncle's, you can feel that there is nothing keeping you in any place but the person beside you with the controls, and a little dip or a little rise can change everything.

Right now, I am watching a cloud disperse and disappear. It's pulled apart by the air until it's nothing. Cotton candy strands that get farther and farther from each other until they dissolve into sugar in between fingers. In between lips.

Our lives are just like this—strings that slip in between realities like a weaving. There is a me somewhere who was overcome by her sadnesses—any of the many—and didn't thrive. There is a me who was a little late to preschool that day and ended up in the crash instead of my friend, Sylvia. There is a me who went to journalism school. There is a me who left the states. There is a childless me, a married me, a blond, brunette, redheaded me. We weave between each other without ever crossing paths. And in my brain, I craft the continuity to make it all one person. All one cloud. That will be pulled apart slowly by the wind and dissolved into molecules.

The clouds float on in the blue sky. I am the same and free to step into any one of my woven paths. Free even to shift vertically to something new.

Knots

When you know how to tie them, they stay.
Through immense pressure, weight, pull,
they get stronger the more you agitate,
When you know how to tie them.

But some knots slip right out when you aren't looking, and you fall.
Some take just one pull of a string
and the ribbon is undone.

Some come undone in your hands, and all the beads crash to
the floor.
You have to know how to tie them—how to interlace and wrap and
when to pull—
to tie them.

And some knots still
are tied quickly and recklessly.
They are a knot on top of a knot—
an accident
a headphone cord
a drawstring—
and no amount of pick or pull or patience will ever open the strands.
They are knotted together forever.

I tie my knots—
one to ten, and again,

stumbling upon an accident—
a rubber band caught in the strands.
I know how to tie some of them,
and for the others, I send up an asking
that they tighten with agitation
over time.

On Lightness

I had a nightmare last night that I was being hunted, and I had no good place to hide. In the dream, I was a different woman, and I only had one child. In the dream, we put a hundred locks on the door and still felt like we were in a glass house. Every crevice I tried to stuff us in felt too exposed. I woke up panicked and didn't want to move. I needed a glass of water, but I lay there staring at the ceiling and waiting for the feeling to pass. Because they all pass, and I have been teaching myself to wait. To pause. To breathe.

All I have in me tonight is just a sentence or two. Barely. I want to show up for myself every day, but today, I did an amazing job of showing up for *them*. I said YES to my toddler when he asked me to play. I said YES to my oldest when he wanted to tell me every single detail of his school day. I said YES to my daughter when she wanted to cuddle me a few minutes longer before bed. I said YES to my baby when she just wanted me to hold her all afternoon. Yes to my children. All day. And it felt good. I laughed. I was light. I remember just last year thinking I would never be light again, but here it was! I stumbled upon levity again. I am smiling again. That's all I have in me tonight.

My Fighter

Here lies my fighter. I've bet on her big. I expect her to win because she always does. Even when she's losing, she will look out at the crowd and declare that it's really a win, that they can't see it, but she is actually winning in some other way. The crowd boos, but she's still winning.

I put all my money on her. She gets stuck in the ring with bigger and bigger opponents that are out of her weight class, that have more deadly weapons, that know her weaknesses and have studied how to beat her. When I watch her, I can't always tell if it's an act when she's down. Sometimes I think she'll stay down. But that rowdy woman gets up and goes again and again. She never stays down and takes it. She's up and fighting. I always leave with the winnings.

But now she is laying down her gloves. She's climbed out of the ring and right into my chest.

There, she curls up inside me and says, "I'm done."

Inside me, it doesn't feel like defeat. More like a job well done. She has fought them all, everything she's ever been up against. People, situations, feelings, imagined threats in the shadows of the night, real threats in her very own home. She's done her job. Now she's taking her epsom salt bath inside my body, and she's leaving the rest to me.

I have taken up acceptance in her absence. I'm betting on it big. Accepting that others are who they are. Accepting that they are not me, do not love like me, do not get angry like me, do not need the same things I need, and cannot know anything about me other than what I allow them to see.

I am accepting that the universe is governed by things we cannot see, and even our best intentions ripple out into spaces we don't intend, and I accept that I cannot know what I am affecting at all times, and I cannot control how I am received, and I cannot force the uncomfortable away, because it will come back every time.

With my fighter at rest, I am opening to anything. There is no good or bad. Hot and cold can both feel the same. They can both feel like just an extreme. Pain and joy can both feel the same. *This is what I have confused about love.*

When I close my eyes and feel compassion for someone's pain in as deep a way as I can, it is a sting. Like a bee. In the center of my chest. I call this sting "love." When I am endeared to someone because of their struggle and I see them trekking uphill and being swallowed by snow over and over again, it is a sting—"love." I have made wild decisions following the trail from this sting. I have deployed my fighter to fight for someone else's pain. It's not her job, and none of it is love.

Acceptance. It's what I'm leading with. It's how I'm working to redefine love. It's how I'm working to redefine fighting. For others and for myself. I will protect my tender heart by accepting everything. Nothing is out of reach. Nothing is shunned. It's all as it should be.

Grounded in My Own Secret Language

Today in yoga, as I meditated, I thought about how unfair my situation is. I'm someone who has sought beautiful, romantic, true love. I have put myself behind the pursuit and given everything I have to my commitment to others, but here I sit anyway with a broken heart. It is unfair that it is broken.

I have always desired a deep connection with another. I have always desired a secret language, a secret code, a secret wink, a secret touch under a table, an intimacy with another that thickens with each year. I have desired a soul connection.

What I've missed is the connection to my own soul, that has already been thickening each year.

I have been whispering to myself, but I haven't listened.
I have been holding myself, but I haven't stopped to feel it.
It can seem lonely when you think that you are your own usher through all the hard times, but the loneliness dims when you recognize that you will never truly abandon yourself.

Even if I plug my ears and refuse to hear my own wisdom, I can never *really* leave myself behind.

I will be here, always, waiting for me to come home.

The Beach Part 5

These beaches feel like mine now. I have accumulated memories of each of them. They have listened to my secrets when I've called them out to the crabs underfoot and the stars above in the middle of a flashlight fight with the kids. I've flown some rich man's kite while he ran up to his mansion to refresh his drink. I've collected a gallon bucket of seashells for my son to smash on his ninth birthday. ("The only thing I want for my birthday is to take a hammer to a pile of seashells.") I have asked the ocean for things to happen in my life, and she has listened and delivered. Perhaps I should have asked her more discriminately, but she listened nonetheless.

Later I would marry on the beach. I would come out during a tropical storm and watch the surfers. I would drink endless coffees in the middle of the afternoon with my toes in the waves. I would bring my family in the winter, my friends in the summer. I would find horseshoe crabs, jellyfish, sand dollars, beadlet anemones, conchs still inside their swirly shells, more hermit crabs, starfish, dolphins, and all the birds. I would never overlook a plover. I would hire a photographer to capture me walking straight out to sea, my dress half soaked, my hands on my swollen stomach, and my skin glowing with the pregnancy of my third child, and then again with my fourth. I would hire a babysitter so I could come out by myself at night and watch the black ocean keep her secrets to herself. I would promise to keep a few of my secrets to myself, to honor myself and only myself as their sole keeper. I would dance and dance and dance in the sand.

Love Poem To Me by Me

Dear Ama,

When I show up on your doorstep, ready to love you all the way,
I will bring pockets of love letters I have written for you, full of all
the small moments I've witnessed and loved about you when you
were busy
because you are so busy.

I will make sure I see you and I write you down
so you can remember that *someone* saw you
when you couldn't.

I will be wearing a coat with way too many pockets, and each one
will be full of letters, and my handwriting will be fast and sloppy
because I love you so much, I will barely have time to get it all out
before the next love comes.

When I show up on your doorstep, it will be with hands ready
to hold a baby and take a toddler outside. It will be with endless
attention and time, and steadiness to hold space for you when you
start to fall apart, because I know you have been waiting for a pocket
to fall apart in.

It will be with a broom to push you out the door and make you
leave and not come back until you've had a full day of sitting on
park benches and crying all the tears you need to cry, and drinking

all the coffee and flirting with all the men and seeing the moon and stars rise up over the black ocean. I will not let you come back here until your cheeks are streaked with mascara and your lips have been kissed by at least one overcome lover and your pockets are full of sand.

When I show up on your doorstep, it will be with a camera to capture you with your children. I will take pictures that you will look at and scoff, I'm sure, because I know that you will first think of yourself as older than you've ever been and so exhausted with circles under your eyes.

But the next day, you will look at the pictures of you with your children and clutch them to your chest and remark on how beautiful they are. Because they show your real life, and they show that someone sees it as a poem and worth capturing and worth printing, and worth holding.

Dear Ama,

I will show up with a reminder that holding someone else's hand through their pain will not fix the parts of you that feel you have been abandoned through your own.

I will show up with a gift, wrapped in delicate lace and golden bows. The gift will be the full power of your broken heart. I will hold you while you open it. You can look at it as long as you need and hold it in your hands too. Use it to honor your past hopes and honor the you that made your mistakes, because you did it from the purity of your loving heart. Then when you have sat with it as long as you need, I will help you churn it down into fertile soil so you can use it to bloom.

I will show up with flowers. Full, huge, colorful flowers with the brightest and biggest petals to remind you to bloom.

Family Judicial Court

I met you in that quiet, clean hallway. You were late. Everything was soundproof, with soundproof doors and insulation that muffled all words. The hallway felt like a blanket wrapped around me. The white chairs and benches weren't stained by pizza fingers. There weren't tiny piles of dirt in the corners. Everything was meticulously wiped down and vacuumed and so quiet. The letters on the door shone gold through fresh Windex—*Family Judicial Court*.

You walked in, and the first thing I noticed was that one of your shoes was untied. The second thing I noticed was a rip in the back of your pants. At first glance, you were put together—your shirt with a collar, your beard trimmed, but there were things slightly askew. They reminded me how much I used to love you. I used to love your quirks. I used to love the way you couldn't keep track of time, the way you floated through life. I used to love your dirty, untied shoes. I used to love your dirty, ripped pants. I still love them.

You wouldn't look at me in that big hallway. You stared down at your phone. You had on a smile, and I knew you were disappearing into the internet. So I played word games until I won them all. I picked at my nails, and the little chips of nail polish fell to the floor, a small token that someone had sat there with nothing left to do with their hands.

Inside the courtroom, everyone had a specific seat, and I didn't know what any of the seats meant. Which one was the security guard? What was the role of the man behind me? I sat where my lawyer told me to.

When the judge was reviewing our agreement, my heart was about to betray me. I could feel it swelling up in my chest. No matter how much of me was committed to this separation, no matter how much I knew it was the right thing to do, my heart was still swelling over and ready to explode.

I felt the tears starting in my pumping heart and lifting up into my chest and my shoulders. Then they were right there behind my eyes, ready for me to let go, ready for me to start sobbing. "Shhh!" I told my tears, and I held them tightly in my chest until they fizzled. I did not let myself cry.

Lately, you have been telling me how detached I am—how cold.
If only you could see how raw and red my flesh is.
If only you could have seen that through our entire relationship, I had absolutely no skin at all—that everything was always exposed as you cut into me over and over—you would know that the detachment, the coldness, is required now.

It is necessary to hold myself here so that you don't see me cry and collect my tears for your poison arrows.

It is necessary to hold my tears, to look like I am cold.

As the judge was silently reading our agreement, the pages made the quietest rip noise when she turned them. Everyone in the courtroom was still and quiet, as if they were all collectively meditating. The man on my right was looking down at his shoes, unmoving. I looked across my lawyer at you, and you were watching the judge with your hands in your lap. It was as if time had stopped with the exception of the paper turning in that woman's hands.

I saw the judge up there in her robe on a pedestal that looked like a throne, with everyone granting her so much reverence, and I wondered how people become judges. What had that small woman done in her life to deserve such respect? People had to ask to approach her. People had to say "if it pleases the court" when they requested something. And by court, they meant her. Who was she? And what would I have to do to be held in the mind that way? What would I have to do to be respected so much that everyone around me defended my right to that respect and protected it? That three men with unclear roles would look at their shoes when I was reading and give me time to think.

Then the judge asked us to stand, and it was as if a hand came from her podium and placed me, small, in front of her. She made us stand for what felt like an eternity in my heels—when was the last time I wore heels? For our entire relationship, I was barefoot at the beach, or barefoot cleaning the house, or barefoot chasing kids.

Before our marriage, I used to wear heels all the time. I used to *work* some high-heel boots, some short minidresses. But in the last three years, I'd forgotten to wear my weapons.

Today I'd worn my weapons, and they were hurting me more than anyone else as I stood there in front of the judge. She asked us questions—I don't remember any of them. I said yes to them. You said, "Yes, ma'am." After a few questions, I wondered if I should also say ma'am. Was I unintentionally showing disrespect? But if I started saying ma'am, would it be an open acknowledgment that I was intentionally disrespecting? Would it be showing you that you may have been right? I stuck with yes, and you stuck with yes ma'am, and I tried not to shift in my heels.

When she asked you why you were accepting such little visitation with your children, you stumbled. Then, eventually, you said, "It seems like something I can't screw up." My lawyer looked at me and rolled her eyes as if you'd said something stupid. But I felt the tears again, and I felt like all the men in the room nodded their heads. It was in my imagination, right? That all of the men felt your honesty? That what you were *really* saying was how you had messed everything up with us beyond repair and that you just didn't want to mess up with our kids, so you'd accepted this visitation schedule, which was barely any visitation, so you could do one thing right? Was it an admittance, in that reverent space, that you knew how bad you'd treated us?

The tears were thinking about escaping, so I focused on my lawyer's rolled eyes. It was a stupid thing to say, not a loving one.

I have had to trust other people's judgment many times throughout this divorce because mine has put me in danger and kept me in danger and slowly washed me away. For whatever reason, I've allowed it to take me. I have had to trust others to bring me back.

I left you in that quiet, clean hallway. Your shoes made no noise as you walked quickly ahead of us, past my nail polish on the floor, through the doors with their gold flourish—*Family Judicial Court*.

Afterward, I met a friend and her son for lunch downtown. The lunch went long. It took me a while to share my true feelings about court, and then it took a while for her son to finish his eggs, and then I got food to go, and finally we walked out, about two hours later.

The day had turned beautiful, and I was admiring the sky, until I saw my car on a tow truck.

I had blocked the driveway of an older woman and kept her from a doctor's appointment. As I ran across the street, food in my arms, purse flapping, they were staring me down.

The parking cop woman had her arms crossed.
The older woman had her arms crossed.
"Didn't you see my car?" the woman said.

"I wasn't looking. I wasn't thinking" I said. I apologized to her over and over again.

"I'm sorry. I'm so sorry. I'm truly sorry. I wasn't looking. I was trying to pay attention, but I couldn't pay attention. I'm sorry".

And then the tears flooded me. They rose *so quick*, too quick for me to swallow them down. Too quick for me to hold them back. I couldn't do anything but stand there and cry
and cry
and cry.

I just came from court, I told them.
From this hallway where there was no sound. From a room where he wouldn't even look at me. From standing in these heels and being worried that my yes wasn't enough.
I cried
and cried
and cried.

The older woman hugged me. The parking cop wrapped her arms around us both.

"I have four kids," I said. "They're babies. They're so young. He is barely going to see them. I don't know how I can do this."

"Tell yourself out loud you're beautiful," one of them said. "Look at yourself in the mirror and tell yourself how proud of yourself you are. Say the words until they become the truth. Put on makeup even when you have nowhere to go, and prance around your house and say you are doing amazing. Focus on yourself and your kids. Give yourself up to a higher power."

Their voices wrapped me up just like their arms.

"You're going to be okay. Your kids are going to be okay."

"That'll be $150," the tow truck man said.
"Oh, here's your parking ticket," the parking cop said.

Succulents

My mother bought me a pot of succulents that have little spiky teeth parts that make them look like mouths. These tiny green plants are so small and fragile
and disguising themselves as violence.

On Grace

In yoga, I used to choose "grace" as my word to invoke before class. I took it to mean ease in the difficult poses. I was going to find grace and ease when my legs were shaking or when my breath was unsteady. That's what I took it to mean.

But what it means now, after this breaking apart of my marriage and this turning away—both from my ex-husband and from myself—is to give myself the understanding I need in all things.

I know why I chose him. I know why I stayed with him. I know why I asked my children to love him.

And I forgive myself in all of the moments where I turned away from myself. And I promise myself I won't do it again.

I give myself grace—
when my legs are shaking and when my breathing is unsteady and when I make mistakes and when I stay too long and when I grieve the loss (even when the thing I lost was killing me) and when I have finally had enough and turn my back for good.
Grace.

Caught

In the beginning, my soul was high. It floated above my body. It shimmered and shook and was full of flow. It flew.

Covid had shut the whole world down. The roads were empty, and my children spun circles in the backyard. They made secret tunnels in the dirt for their toys. We were getting grocery deliveries and wiping every box off with Clorox wipes and washing our hands. We were yelling hello to our friends from our doorstep as they drove by just to say hi. I met a boy online, and he came over to give me a kiss, but then wiped his lips and counted ten days before he'd consider coming back again. Everything could have felt isolating. Everything could have felt so lonely. But—

My soul was high. My soul collected my tiny young soul-lings and flew us straight to the ocean every day, past the barricades, past the police that had closed the shore. I snuck us down to stick our toes in the waves, and my soul floated high above us in a bright mischievous shine. We were breaking rules to touch what should always be free, and my soul was elated.

I was dancing during this time.
I would dance in the living room and in the kitchen with my children. I would dance on my phone. I danced in bed.

Dance created space in all the tiny crevices inside my body. It freed any bit of pain I was hiding, which means sometimes I would cry.

But when I would cry, my soul would shimmer and get a little higher.
So, in the beginning, my soul was high.

My soul had long strands of pearls.
My soul had seashell strings that floated in the wind.
My soul trailed up and out like Medusa's hair.
My soul was not contained.
One Tuesday at sunset, my soul's seashell strands of shimmer and
swirl got caught on the toes of a warrior.

He was walking by, and I was so open wide, and right around the tip
of his pinkie toe, I was caught and dragged along the sandy beach.

It was fine at first. Just sandy, with bits of beach in the cracks and
crevices of my car and in my hair. I was picking out sand from every
corner of my life.

Until my warrior took me to the edge of the beach and walked us
both right into the ocean, past the wave break.

This is when I realized my warrior was made out of stone.

My bright, shiny, seashell soul swam toward the shore. She called
on every bit of air and lightness she could find. She called on wings,
she called on birds, she called on billowing wind, but was dragged
under anyway.

The deep ocean is a corner of the kitchen, stuck up against the
cabinets in a ball. The darkest place in the whole ocean is on the
linoleum floor on New Years Eve, scratching at your chest to set your
heart free. There is only the light from things that are waiting to eat

you, from things that have benefited from looking terrifying or being terrifying or from having no rules but to "devour."

My stone warrior fell down there with my soul wrapped around his toes. Maybe he didn't mean to. Sometimes I think he didn't know he was made of stone—that when he took me out to the ocean, it was because he thought he could float. Other times I think he knew, and went because he wanted to see what would happen when something like me went too.

Would I still be able to shine? Would I still fly?

I thought because he was a warrior, the stone warrior would fight to rise, so I sat in the dark and waited for the weight of him to swim back toward the air.

But I didn't know that warriors are each built for different kinds of battles, and this one was not built to go toward the light.

If you sit in the dark long enough, it will spill in through your skin and start to color the water that lives between your organs. It will be all you see and all you breathe. If you sit in the dark long enough, you become part of it too.

When my warrior didn't stand,
and when I started to become the dark,
some tiny part of the shimmery soul went to work on the
snagged strand.

It picked it apart thread by thread, seashell by seashell, shimmer by shimmer. My soul did it by feel, guided by intuition and memory of being high. She untied herself from the stone warrior and floated us both straight back up to the sun.

Once on land, I gathered her up and stuffed her inside my chest and built walls all around her to keep her safe.

But that won't work either, she says. *That's a different kind of darkness,* she says. *I didn't need grounding by another,* she says. *I was flying so high because I had you(me) as my mast.*

You don't need to hold me here. You don't need the walls. You just need your feet to be strong on the earth, and your soul can be free.
Souls cannot be wounded, she says.
Souls cannot be dimmed.
Even in the deepest, darkest, kitchen-floor ocean, we will pick apart what's holding us under, strand by strand, and find the sky.

The Beach Part 6

It's 9 a.m. on a Wednesday when I take the two littlest ones to the ocean. I set them right down in the sand. The baby smiles so big when she realizes where we are. She stomps her bare feet up and down and runs around in a tiny circle. She finds a little puddle and stands in the center, digging down with her hands. The toddler runs to the biggest rock he can carry, and asks for help throwing it in the waves. We walk together down to the shore, and I pick him up and walk, in my tennis shoes, through the shallow water, so he can throw it into the breaking wave, my socks soggy.

Again and again, another rock, and another.

Eventually, I tell him he can get his own feet wet, and lifting that little boundary gives him pure joy. He runs back and forth from the rocks into the tiny waves that lap at his toes, throwing the rocks in and watching them roll in the waves. The baby sits down right in the puddle. I let them get sandy and wet and cold. I let them run and roll and be free.

My toddler is an explosive child. It's just this last week that I've been saying this out loud. Something about saying it has freed me from expecting him not to be. This expectation has created so much tension. I used to respond in anger and frustration when he would lose control of his body and try to fight me, but this week I have accepted who he is, and it has freed us both.

My beautiful, full, sensitive, opinionated boy who is IN THE WORLD with every foot he has, hands fully covered in dirt, with face showing every single feeling. I do not need to force him to be like the others. I do not need to break his spirit so he's easier for me. Together, through acceptance, we have come closer. He is more trusting of me. I am more loving with him. My explosive child and I are learning each other this way.

At the beach, he is now wet from his feet to his knees, but he is so happy. Why keep him dry anyway? We are by the ocean, and it calls us in, and who am I to say no?

True Love

I take a deep breath and look at the table at Jason's Deli where we are all sitting for dinner.

I am not alone.
I have given this world four extensions of myself, and I pour every day of my life into them, so aware that the days are changing. That one is talking to me less, and one is talking to me more. That one is growing out of their shoes, and the other is giving up naps for good. And before I can fully process this moment or fully taste my salad or fully take it all in, I will look at the table, and they will all be bigger than I am, or it will be just two, or it will just be me.

So here is my love poem
to the four of you together
at my table at Jason's Deli:

I love you all
with an aching heart.
All of you are pure.
So pure it is visceral.
You are the creative expression of each year you were born.
I spent nine months eating the vitamins and putting in the naps and avoiding sushi and dancing
so the water around you could swirl with the sounds outside.
I created space for you.
More and more space for you.

Enough space for you to spin yourselves into gold
so pure
that you now shine with it.

All of you, your long eyelashes.
I cannot stop looking at you
or photographing you by that wall, eating yogurt—hands and fingers
covered in the mess.
Your eyes are beautiful, marbled colors.
Two so blue they must have come straight from the sky.
One a brown like her father.
One a hazel green
for me.
All of you, laughing at each other or kicking each other under the
table, the youngest two are sticky and dripping chocolate.
One with their foot up, snacking on a tomato.
One eating a pizza and a half.
One with a body wiggling back and forth in his chair and—oh no,
he's on the floor.
One with this quiet, calm openness, where does she even get
that calm?

All of you, together, make up the noise of my life.
It is noise that I move to one side when I need to make space for my
own thoughts, or
noise that overtakes me when the door opens at 3,
or noise that I close my eyes and try to remember to hold
in some distant place in my brain.
To hold so close
because you are all already out of my arms, even the baby is out of
my arms,

you're all sitting around this table like a family.
I've made an entire family.

I created space for you.
More and more space for you.
Enough space for you to spin yourselves into gold
so pure
that you will shine with it for good.

TRY

Ten years ago, on a sleeping-bag-sheet, after freeing my hands from rope tied to the anvil in the middle of the floor, I wiped the mascara off my cheeks and sighed with relief. I closed my eyes.

It was always when my eyes were closed that he talked the most, as if under the scrutiny of the certain color yellow my irises become, nothing could get done. But once closed—

He told me everything as I drifted in and out of sleep. He told me about everyone, about his fists and who they'd hit, how much it cost to get the right kind of drunk, family dogs, family shit, girlfriends he wished he could still taste, girlfriends he wished he could quit, the names of medicines recited like incantations, and somewhere around 4 a.m., he stopped and cried and said, "I'm going to hurt you, I'm going to hurt you, I'm going to hurt you."

I rolled over and steadied myself. At the time, I was so.fucking.steady.
I said, "You can't."
He said, "I can! I can and I'm going to. I'm going to hurt you."
And I said, "You can't."
I said, "Try."

Fresh from death, my dad's body was in a cardboard box under my stepmother's bed. What that does to you, I still can't say, but I knew nothing could hurt me the way my dad dying did, and life was *exquisite*.

He could have lined his exes up in the room with us, and I would have gone down the line and bit their lips with kisses until we were all cherry-apple red.

My dad gave me the most beautiful experience I've ever had: freedom. He opened up the whole universe for me. Anything I wanted, I could have. I was particle matter. I was the energetic release in his eyes the moment he took his last breath.

I couldn't be hurt by any failure, any lover, anything at all.

The Beach Part 7

I think often about how my father loved the beach, but I haven't held onto a single memory of going with him. I have pictures of him smiling brightly while burying his friends in the sand, body surfing the waves, deep-sea fishing. I dig and dig in my past for any moment I remember of walking on the beach with him, or playing in the waves. There's nothing. There is only the memory of his death bed, of the moment he's trying to die, and of my stepmother's voice telling him he should find his rocking chair where he can sit and look out at the beach like he always dreamt of doing. She's telling him how she will meet him there.

It's 9 a.m. on a Saturday, and I go back to the beach. I take all four of them and set them free. I watch the waves and sand kiss over and over again, both giving and taking, sometimes equally and sometimes catastrophically. I'll hold you. I'll fill you. I'll take what I want. I'll give back what I can.

The Lightness of Being Grounded

I plant my feet down into the earth and close my eyes to find
my roots.
They are small little things.
A breeze could blow me right over.
But I love the wind, and I invite it in.

I welcome it, even as it threatens to uproot me.
I open my arms, and I feel the terror, and I say,
Thank you.

I need the wind to deepen the roots.
I need the wind to grow.
Thank you.
More.

The more I am shaken up,
the deeper I will ground,
the higher I will rise
to touch that crisp sunrise sky.

Epilogue

The words in this book were written in the middle of my terrible separation. My marriage was rough, and my separation was rougher, and it is not an exaggeration to say that the breakdown is all I thought about day and night for months.

What I see when I read these pieces is an honest account of my experience in the in-between place. I see myself with the rug pulled out from under me, struggling to make sense of it and trying to reconcile my heartbreak with my guilt for allowing something so wrong to go on so long. I see myself floating through the grief.

What I also see is that my path through the grief emerged, woven through each piece, and that it got wider and clearer and stronger the more I wrote—as if the only way to find it was to write this book.

The only way to find my light again was to ground down.

Ground down into the earth, into what I knew to be true about myself, into the future I wanted to create, and into the love I had for myself. (I had to really dig for a while to find that one, but it was there. It's the taproot.)

More than once (a day) during the editing process, I wanted to scrap everything I'd written. It's incredibly difficult to go back and read how lost I was, especially when I know the ending—that I'm going to find myself. I've come so far since writing these pieces.

But my hope for this book is that it lands in the laps of those who are in the in-between and that it can serve as a companion. I hope these stories sit beside them when they, too, cannot see how in the hell they're ever going to plant their feet down into the earth again. I hope finding my way through can help them find theirs.

About the Author

Ama is a writer, mother, and artist. She studied contemporary dance at the University of North Carolina School of the Arts and believes dancing and writing are intertwined. She penned her first novel in the summer of 1999 in a college-ruled composition book, and in the twenty-five years since, she's managed multiple online blogs, released a zine-to-mail series called *The Glitch*, a story-to-mail series called "White," and started a small press publishing company called Aproprose Press. She likes seeing her work in paper over digital and is happiest when that paper is being dog eared and underlined. She currently lives in Charleston, South Carolina, with her four children.